THE
HAGGLER'S
HANDBOOK

ONE HOUR TO
NEGOTIATING POWER

THE HAGGLER'S HANDBOOK

ONE HOUR TO NEGOTIATING POWER

Leonard Koren & Peter Goodman

W·W· NORTON & COMPANY · NEW YORK · LONDON

First published as a Norton paperback 1992

Book and jacket design by Leonard Koren; icon design by Leonard Koren and Taki Ono; typesetting by Harrington-Young Typography & Design, Albany, California

Library of Congress Cataloging-in-Publication Data

Koren, Leonard
*   The Haggler's Handbook: one hour to negotiating power / Leonard Koren & Peter Goodman.*
*   p.   cm.*
*   Includes index.*
*   I. Negotiation.   I. Goodman, Peter.   II. Title.*
*   BF637.N4K67   1991*
*   158'.5—dc20*   *90–28106*

ISBN 0–393–30920–7

W. W. Norton & Company, Inc., 500 Fifth Avenue, New York, N.Y. 10110
W. W. Norton & Company Ltd, 10 Coptic Street, London WC1A 1PU

*   5 6 7 8 9 0*

CONTENTS

CHAPTER 2

Basic Psychology

CHAPTER 3

Short Negotiations

CHAPTER 4

Longer Negotiations

CHAPTER 5

More Formal Negotiations: Contracts, Consultants, and Bureaucracies

CHAPTER 6

What to Do at an Impasse

CHAPTER 7

Dirty Tactics and Strategies

● INTRODUCTION

Many of us think negotiating with a car salesman is worse than root canal work without Novocain. We look at "standard contracts" and sign them without thinking. When asked to name a price, we do so—and end up settling later for much less.

So we try to avoid such painful situations. In reality, however, human interaction is in large part nothing but a series of negotiated agreements. We negotiate with our kids about the family vacation. We persuade our friends to go with us to such and such a restaurant for dinner. We try to get the dry cleaner to make amends for that scorched white shirt. These small-scale agreements we make every day are the essence of our civilization: they moderate our primitive selfish desires—and in the end they probably keep us from killing each other.

The premise of *The Haggler's Handbook* is that if you have to negotiate every day of your life, you may as well be good at it and get what you want. We've called our book a "haggler's" handbook because "haggling" sounds more personal and recreational (and a little more quarrelsome) than "negotiating," which smacks of the boardroom and starched collars.

Having a sense of humor is important here, because **conscious negotiation is a game**. Not taking yourself too seriously—learning to stay loose—makes you a more effective player.

The Haggler's Handbook offers a smorgasbord of negotiating options—some 130 tips, tactics, and strategies. These are timeless principles that will work just as well in the rug bazaar as in the corporate tower. What we've done with these principles is put them in a convenient form for your quick reference and use.

Because every negotiating situation is different and needs a different approach, you'll find that some of the strategies we propose are contradictory. We've used icons to indicate whether a particular tactic is best suited for **cooperative** (win-win), **competitive** (cutthroat), or **in-between** negotiating postures.

Which strategy is best? Partly that depends on who you are. Can you play hardball? Can you stomach the anxiety that comes with classic ploys like the bluff or take-it- or-leave-it?

A lot of you can't—and good for you! Because the most powerful deals are those in which both parties emerge feeling they've gained something of value. People who make win-win deals feel good about themselves *and* will work to make sure the deal goes through—by selling it to their colleagues and by smoothing out any hitches that may arise later.

But what if your opponent is not as charitable as you? The more aggressive ideas in this book will prepare you for the worst sleazeball you can imagine. Walk away if you can. But if you can't, use these ideas to bury him before he buries you.

• HOW TO USE THIS BOOK

We know you're a busy person, so we've devised a format that will let you acquire the negotiating skills you need quickly. The book is organized into seven chapters, covering first the general preparation and psychology of negotiating and then the different situations you may find yourself in: short negotiations, protracted negotiations, stalled negotiations, and negotiations with professionals, bureaucrats, and dirty players.

Read through the book once—we figure it'll take you about an hour. On each page is a different negotiating concept. An **icon** identifies the entry by confrontation level. The **trigger words** will call up the concept in your memory and can also be used when referring to the Contents. Next is the **entry number**. At the center of the page in boldface type is a succinct statement of the **negotiating concept**. In the box is an **explanation of the concept** in detail with examples and cautionary notes. At the bottom of the page is the **chapter title**.

After you've read through the entries, you can refer back to them quickly for ideas on how to approach a particular situation or opponent. Since this book is small enough to hide under your coat, if you find yourself in a jam, call a break (a trip to the bathroom, for example) and use the time to scan the trigger words in the Contents to refresh your memory.

You'll find that skill in negotiating will benefit you in many different ways. It will give you more self-confidence. It will increase your standing at work. But most important it will give you more control over your life. Now *you* set the terms. *You* make the deals. *You* reap the rewards.

competitive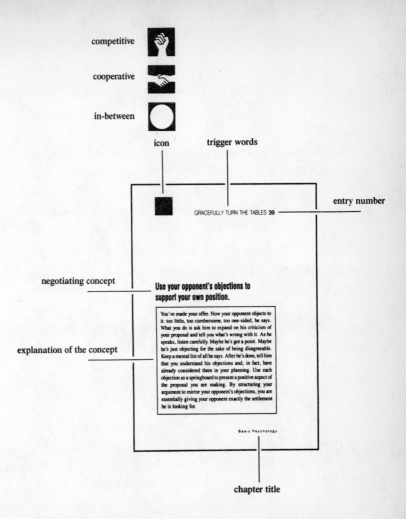

cooperative

in-between

icon   trigger words

entry number

negotiating concept

Use your opponent's objections to support your own position.

explanation of the concept

You've made your offer. Now your opponent objects to it: too little, too cumbersome, too one-sided, he says. What you do is ask him to expand on his criticism of your proposal and tell you what's wrong with it. As he speaks, listen carefully. Maybe he's got a point. Maybe he's just objecting for the sake of being disagreeable. Keep a mental list of all he says. After he's done, tell him that you understand his objections and, in fact, have already considered them in your planning. Use each objection as a springboard to present a positive aspect of the proposal you are making. By structuring your argument to mirror your opponent's objections, you are essentially giving your opponent exactly the settlement he is looking for.

Basic Psychology

chapter title

One final note: the masculine pronoun "he" is used throughout for brevity and consistency. But we want to emphasize that the ideas here belong to no sex or class of person, and are meant to empower all people in all walks of life.

CHAPTER 1

Preparation

Read and remember everything in this book.

The one who wins the war isn't always the strongest. It's often the one who's smartest, most creative, and in possession of the best information. Study the powerful ideas in this book so you can draw on them at the negotiating table. They'll teach you when to cooperate, when to attack, when to flee, and when to parry and stall for time. Mix and match these ideas to create an arsenal of negotiating styles and techniques. With dozens of gambits at your disposal, you won't have to lock into any one tactic. Stay flexible and alert—because you never know what your opponent is going to do.

"Know thyself." Understand your needs, assumptions, and beliefs.

Because we're all different, all of us are going to approach life—and negotiations—in a different way. Some people value money and power. Some people want to win. Some people just want justice. It all depends on personal style and values, but two things are for sure: (1) you'll never get what you want if you don't know what you're looking for, and (2) you're dead if your opponent understands you better than you understand yourself. On a piece of paper, write down the five things most important to you. Now ask a friend to also write down five things he thinks are important to you. Do the lists match up? How might an opponent try to use those perceived motivations against you? Are you going to be fighting for honor, when in fact what you want is money, or vice versa? Try to perceive where you are most vulnerable—and protect yourself.

"Know thy opponent." Find out all you can about the person you'll be dealing with.

Most people are predictable. They have a certain style they bring to everything they do, including negotiating. Before talking to your opponent, talk to his friends, his enemies, and people who have negotiated with him before. Listen to gossip and industry scuttlebutt. Find out where he lives, in what neighborhood, in what kind of house, so you can visualize him better. Even try calling up your competitors for clues to what your opponent's after and whether he's tough or bluff. Then sit down and make a list of what you know and what it might mean for your negotiations. EXAMPLE: Family and health are two big motivators. Does your opponent have relatives he wants to provide for, or a health problem that makes it imperative he settle quickly?

Cultivate a detached attitude toward the outcome of the negotiation.

Banish from your mind the idea that everything—your home, your bank account, your job—depends on your negotiating skill. Negotiating is a game, and to do it well you have to have a sense of fun, an appreciation for the thrill of the hunt. Worry too much and you get nervous and easy to trip up. Don't fret about inconsequential details along the way—keep your eyes on the prize. USEFUL: Deep breathing, mental exercises where you visualize yourself winning, and a full-body massage are all good ways of relaxing before a meeting.

Be patient.

What's your hurry? Overeagerness makes it appear you really want something, and to the extent you reveal you want it your opponent will try to withhold it from you. Stalling for time lets you focus on the issues, not the people involved or your sense of obligation for the big meal you've just enjoyed at their expense. If you can't think of the right thing to do—do nothing and wait and see what happens tomorrow. Remember: In business, what counts is what you end up with, not how quickly you get it. OUNCE OF PREVENTION: Never take your checkbook or credit cards to the car dealership or when you're seriously "just looking."

Be persistent.

Keep at it. Your strategy may fail the first time, but you can always come back and try again. The important thing is to keep on top of current events and *know* when the situation has changed in your favor. TRUE STORY: Ed, a San Francisco man, sees a house he wants to buy. It's not listed, but Ed's realtor discovers the elderly ladies who own it will sell for $350,000. So Ed offers what *he* thinks it's worth, or $220,000. The ladies refuse, and are insulted by Ed's low offer. Ed instructs his realtor to call the ladies periodically to renew the offer anyway. Then the earthquake of October 1989 hits, and the ladies, very shaken up, call Ed's realtor. Ed closes the deal for $220,000.

Be willing to take risks.

Negotiation is a process. Between the action and the result is a span of time we call the Risk Zone. It's the period right after you call your opponent's bluff and before you see if your ploy worked. It's the time when you've turned down one offer to buy your car and you're waiting for the better offer you think is out there. It can be nerve-wracking, and that's why some people try to narrow the Risk Zone. But sometimes these people end up narrowing the Reward. To the extent you can handle the tension, broaden the Risk Zone. BAD EXAMPLE: A collector turns down a good offer for a stamp, and then loses his nerve overnight. He calls his opponent in the morning saying he'll take his offer—not realizing that the bidder was just about to call *him* with a better deal.

Don't be bashful: try to get everything your heart desires.

You're not a bad person just because you want what you want. You're not being selfish when you refuse to concede a point that matters to you. A lot of people feel awkward when making their initial pitch, as if they're asking for more than they really deserve (or expect to get). Their eyes dart around, their voices drop in volume, and their opponent immediately gains the upper hand. You don't have to ask for everything the first time out, but you do have to believe that it's fundamentally OK to want what you want. THE POINT: You're the one who's got to live with the deal when it's done.

Hone your ability to bluff, mug, and act.

Maybe the world isn't a stage, but it helps to pretend it is. Here are some tactics to practice. (1) The Poker Face: don't let on when you're upset, frightened, delighted, confused. Practice looking spiritually unruffled. (2) The converse of this, or the Mug: use your face to express outrage, disbelief, scorn, power. (3) The Bluff: the classic ploy whose effectiveness can be heightened by a deft use of (1) and (2). TIP: Look your opponent in the eye when performing; it'll make you seem more natural and sincere.

The more important the negotiation, the more research you need.

How much preparation you do for a negotiation depends on what's riding on the deal. Never walk into a situation blind, understanding only your own goal—the particular price you're willing to pay, for example. Postpone the negotiation if you have to, but take the time to become an expert on the subject you'll be working on. Go to the library and check out the industry reports. Talk to other professionals, particularly academics who are masters of the industry overview and who will expound at the drop of a hat. Study your opponent's company, its reputation, its financial position, its market share. If you care about the result, you have to care about the preparation.

Start negotiating even *before* you "start negotiating," when your opponent is off guard and relaxed.

If there's something you want, don't just call up cold and start negotiating for it. Establish an informal communication level first. Chat about this and that, and merely touch on the subject of real interest to you. Give away good (but not vital) information in the hope of getting good (and vital) information in return. Then let the subject drop until you talk again next time. Once you're in the negotiating room and your opponent feels he's got to look tough in front of his minions, it won't be so easy to have a friendly exchange.

Remember: your opponent will be researching *your* weak points too.

On the negotiating highway, practice defensive driving. Assume your opponent has found out that you're in debt, that you've never done a really big deal before, or that you're not a math whiz. Take precautions: (1) hide what you can, (2) prepare useful spins about the things you cannot hide, (3) talk to your friends before your opponent does, (4) hire an expert to advise you in the areas you don't entirely understand, (5) train yourself to pause and think before speaking.

Figure out the most you could hope to gain from the negotiation.

What's the best you could possibly do in a negotiation? No, not what you'll settle for, but what you could expect if everything goes your way? As your opening position, this is what you should ask for. Asking big gives you confidence, and it lets your opponent know you're not a pushover. Also, negotiating is a horse trade—you probably won't get your opening position. One thing's for sure, though: you won't get more than what you ask for. EXAMPLE: Honest Ed was selling his boat and asked for what he thought it was worth, considering it needed repainting. His opponent immediately asked for a reduction—because the boat needed a new paint job!

Ask big, but don't jack up your position beyond reason.

Your opponent should know from the outset that you're not crazy or greedy but have simply done your homework. Start out with too high a demand and he will immediately show you why your position is untenable, thus undermining any future strategy you might employ. Instead ask big, but build support for your position with relevant documents (reports, receipts, blueprints, and the like), evidence of other offers, and any other hard information you can gather.

When there are many issues to be decided in a negotiation, rank your goals in order of relative importance.

Know what you want, but also know what you'll give up to get it. Say you've been offered a job, and with it comes a package of benefits, many of which are not adequate for you. Which do you care about the most? The health coverage for your growing family? The car? The stock options? Your title? The location of your office? Would you be willing to forgo the job if some or all of the benefits weren't changed? If health care and job title matter most, focus on these and be willing to compromise on the rest. SUGGESTION: Compromising doesn't mean giving up, it means being creative. For example, you can make certain parts of your final agreement provisional, say for a year, after which they will be renegotiated.

Figure out what your options are if negotiations fail. What's the very *least* you'll settle for?

Knowing that you have other options makes you a much more powerful negotiator. Say you want to sell your company. Before talking to your main prospect, talk to his competitors and see if they might be interested too. What happens if you simply sell the real estate and walk away? What if you hang on and groom a successor to take over in a few years? Explore each option on paper. Look at its financial implications. Now look at its emotional implications. Use the viability and appeal of these options to help figure out what your minimum negotiating position is going to be.

**Keep what you're least willing
to accept absolutely secret. But
if you have attractive options, let
your opponent know what they are.**

Concealment and disclosure are equally powerful strategies. Never let on (1) that you need the deal or (2) how far you're willing to go to get it. But if you have good options (ones you can really count on), disclose them, so that your opponent knows you can walk away if you feel like it. TACTIC: *You* control the concealment and disclosure of information. Don't respond to direct questions, unless your answer will advance your position.

**Plan your strategy carefully,
but stay flexible and be aware when
the situation and circumstances are
changing.**

Closedmindedness can be deadly. By all means plan for your negotiation. Figure your options. Do your research. But don't let the amount of work you put into your preparations prevent you from seeing new opportunities that the other side might offer you. Before you react to a proposal think: (1) what is my "stock" answer to this? and then (2) what if I go along with the idea? You have to keep your mind active, always sorting through the data. Don't get lost in details, though. Keep your main, larger goals firmly in mind as an anchor.

Ask your friends for help and advice in planning and strategy.

You may be a loner, but negotiation is by definition an interaction between people. So use other people as part of your preparation. Your friends—personal and business—are particularly useful. Their honest perceptions about you and their suggestions for strategy can be most useful. Most important, your friends are on your side. They can offer you encouragement and support when you're feeling threatened. Share your thoughts and feelings with people you love and trust, because your feelings are the true keys to your confidence and success.

Before an important negotiation, prepare a script and practice acting it out.

Lawyers often stage mock trials before going to court. This gives them a chance to polish their arguments and gauge the likely reaction of judge and jury before it's too late to turn back. You can prepare a negotiating script for the same purpose. Try it out with your friends and colleagues, with one person in the role of your hard-nosed opponent. Playacting not only gives you lines and arguments to draw on, but it also trains your emotions to follow a comfortable path around volatile and contentious issues. RECOMMENDATIONS: (1) Don't overpractice; once or twice through a script is enough. (2) Always playact in an unfamiliar room; this creates a tension and uncertainty similar to the real thing.

CHAPTER 2

Basic Psychology

Your opponent will negotiate with you only if he feels tempted or threatened.

There are two tacks you can take with your opponent. You can either say, "This is what you'll get if you make a deal," or you can say, "This is what'll happen to you if you don't." These approaches are complementary. Which one you use, or how you combine them, depends on your assessment of your opponent and what you think motivates him. Is he greedy or scared? COROLLARY: Think carefully about your own desire and fear factors as part of your prenegotiation strategy.

You'll get more out of the negotiation if your opponent likes you.

People like doing business with people they like. They'll concede a point or two if they feel the other guy is basically honest, fair, and friendly. Bluffing, exaggeration, and obfuscation are all a part of the game, but they have to be carried out with a measure of sincerity. Look and act devious, and you build mistrust and resistance. LONG-TERM GAIN: Lots of deals don't end when the contract is signed. You and your "opponent" may now find yourself partners in the enterprise.

Set a pleasant and cooperative tone for the negotiation, and your opponent will respond in kind.

Think of your negotiation as a working relationship, where both of you have the same goal. Avoid confrontation at the outset. Banish the direct, harsh-sounding word "no" from your vocabulary. Start off slow. Make small talk. Find common interests. Show respect (especially to your opponent's staff, who may be more influential than you realize). Building trust and goodwill is not wasting time. When discussions get heated, your good feelings for each other may be all you have holding you together. IN JAPAN: Businessmen spend great amounts of their private time establishing close personal relationships with their clients, playing golf, going out together in the evening, and visiting each other's offices simply to chat. When it comes time for the actual "negotiation," the important matters have already been discussed.

Humanize the proceedings by expressing your feelings, and get your opponent to do the same.

If you're hurt, betrayed, or angry, sometimes the best thing to do is to tell the other side exactly how you're feeling. Putting a lock on your emotions takes effort and can interfere with your ability to think and respond clearly. Tell your opponent: "I left our last meeting feeling you really weren't taking me very seriously. If we're going to get anywhere, you have to treat me better." This tactic often gets the other side to open up and tell you how *they're* feeling too, and can be an important means of establishing trust.

If your opponent is from another culture, be aware of your differences from the outset.

Goals, personal styles, body language, speech, and many other factors that determine the shape of a negotiation differ from culture to culture. Should the laid-back Californian breeze into the office of a high-powered Chicago attorney? Only if he wants to risk making this particular statement a part of his strategy. Understanding is hard enough between people who share basic assumptions. Cultural differences can be a real barrier to progress. WATCH OUT: Don't assume that a fairly fluent non-native speaker of English can follow your fast-paced patter. Slow down. Speak clearly. Repeat. Periodically check for understanding. Also, don't assume that just because your opponent's English is halting that he's not bright enough to beat you. Finally, if you have a choice of languages to negotiate in, always choose your own.

Find and pander to your opponent's emotional needs—but make sure you don't get caught by the same technique.

Use your opponent's emotional needs to reach behind his rational, argumentative mind. If he is a self-made man he may need praise for his accomplishments and flattery to make him feel he really is as good as he's worked to be. An elderly owner selling out may need to feel he's leaving his "family" in responsible hands. A bankrupt entrepreneur wants to believe he's not a failure. Don't overdo it, however. Sometimes a simple conciliatory word or compliment is all it takes to get your opponent on your side. LESSON: Be just as aware of your own emotional needs, and watch out for the other guy trying to do to you what you're doing to him.

Don't diminish your credibility by apologizing or trying to be Mr. Nice Guy.

Never say you're sorry for asking for what you want and need. Your opponent may appreciate your sentiment, but he'll instantly mark you as a softy and try to use your apologetic streak to weaken your resolve. Be polite. But don't back down. Don't make joking, self-deprecating remarks. Don't pause and look away before answering. Don't let your chest sink and your shoulders slouch. Don't change your mind when challenged. Get your opponent to like you, but get him to respect you too.

Never criticize or reject your opponent's position out of hand.

When your opponent is making his pitch, nod your head and offer verbal encouragement as he speaks, indicating you understand (even if you don't agree). Then, when he's done, don't slam back at him with reasons why his offer is bad or unworkable. Instead, mention the points you agree with and how they might fit in to what you're offering. Denouncing your opponent's position forces him to defend it and hold onto it. This leads to a tug of war, not a settlement.

If your opponent throws a tantrum, don't react. Let him get it off his chest.

Sometimes the wisest course is just to sit and wait while your opponent releases all his pent-up fury and frustration. Don't blow back at him—that could get messy. Instead, listen quietly, nod your head, say you understand, and then, when he's done fuming, diffuse his anger by thanking him for speaking so frankly. He'll have gotten whatever's bugging him off his chest (and no one will think him a wimp), and you'll get a reputation for being coolheaded. INSIGHT: There's a great psychological factor here. Just because you listened, your opponent can end up thinking you're his friend and may be eager to give you a better deal.

Put yourself in your opponent's place to understand his point of view.

You're way ahead of the game once you realize that making a deal does not lie in getting your opponent to see things your way but, rather, in getting your opponent to see things *his* way and *still* make the deal. You're not all of a sudden going to turn a miser into a philanthropist. Instead, you've got to look at the deal from the miser's perspective—how much do I get to keep? Before beginning a negotiation, focus on your opponent's needs and avoid projecting your own desires and anxieties onto his. This not only prepares you for things your opponent may say or do, but it also offers you a good starting point for creating a settlement that serves both of you well. If you know what your opponent wants, it might be within your power to give it to him.

Ask your opponent, in a straightforward way, what he wants.

Sometimes you don't have to be cagey. Not every opponent is a master of deceit. You'll find, in fact, that many of the people you deal with don't like playing the negotiation game and would rather just make a quick and simple deal. Some people are so uncomfortable with lying that they will tell the truth, even when they know the truth is not in their best interest. Ask a couple why they're selling their home, and maybe they'll tell you that they found a new place and need the down payment fast. Bingo! You've just knocked $10,000 off the sale price! This is why agents hate to have their clients around on open-house days. And this is why you should get to your opponent when his guard dogs (his lawyers and tax advisors) are absent. Informal situations like parties and meals out offer good opportunities for frank discussion.

Ask lots of questions. Listen carefully to the answers, and *watch* how the answers are given.

You can learn a lot by asking questions, and not just in the obvious way. What's not said is just as important as what is said. If you keep asking about sales figures and your opponent keeps talking about next year's revenues, this should send up a warning flag. Does your opponent suddenly lapse into stilted press-agent jargon when answering a tough question? Does he seem ill at ease? Watch his hands. Does he fidget or drum on the desk? Does he look away? Do his meaning and speech conflict with each other, the one assured, the other full of doubt? All these are important clues to what's really going on. CAUTION: Don't assume that just because your opponent's agitated he's nervous about the negotiations. He may just be a high-strung, overworked executive. COROLLARY: Asking questions and listening prevents you from revealing important and possibly damaging information of your own.

Pretend you know less than you do, and your opponent may tell you more than you need.

This is what one top negotiator calls the Columbo technique, where you act like such an ignoramus that the criminal, in his arrogance, practically hands you himself on a platter. Don't expect negotiations to be as tidy as a TV show, but the psychological gamesmanship is the same: if you act confused, ask a lot of questions, and generally look as if you need a little help with the details, your opponent will be disarmed and may even volunteer the information you need to support your position. TIP: People like to feel they're really in the know—when questioning junior staff and your opponent's customers, always act as if the information they give you is new and useful, even when it's not.

Be an active listener, and let your opponent see that you understand what he is saying.

Pay attention to paying attention. Listen carefully to what your opponent is saying. Follow his line of argument. If you let your mind drift, you may hesitate to ask that a particular point be repeated. But if you're listening carefully, you'll know when it's appropriate to ask questions. Also, you should occasionally offer a reality check, vocalizing your opponent's point of view and asking him whether you've got it right. This clarifies his position, and lets him know that you have been paying attention and taking him seriously. TACTIC: Keep interjecting short affirmative phrases as you listen to your opponent, like "uh-huh," "yes," and "I see." This makes the speaker want to keep talking, and is a good way of eliciting more information.

Put your arguments in terms your opponent can identify with and understand.

Remember the high-school physics teacher who would use the trajectory of a football or the swing of a baseball bat to present the concepts of hard science? The point: people will listen to you if you speak their language. If your opponent is a sports fan, speak in sports analogies. If he's a bean counter, bring your beans. Remember, you may be coming at him with a "foreign" proposition, so it's in your best interests to make it seem familiar and nonthreatening. Draw your opponent into your proposal. Use historical, cooking, and sports analogies—if you don't know any offhand, make a point of finding some as part of your research.

Accentuate the positive, eliminate the negative.

People's first reaction when faced with a proposal to (1) spend money, (2) reorganize, or (3) do anything new— is to say no. Your job is to stress all the good things that will happen if your ideas are accepted. You want a new computer system. Yes, it will cost the firm money. But it will pay for itself in increased efficiency and power. It will run these specific programs, and handle these particular kinds of graphics, and in so doing you will save the company so many dollars in outside labor charges. Who can argue with that? Don't rebut your opponent (your boss in this instance) by telling him that he's wrong or stingy. Keep on an even keel, and think and talk positive.

Give your opponent time to digest new and unfamiliar ideas.

People are threatened by change. They need to get used to the idea that things are going to be different, that they are going to have to pay more, that the contract terms are going to be more stringent than last time. When you have to bring up an unpleasant fact of life in the course of your negotiations, do it early on so that your opponent has a chance to get used to it. Later on, refer to it now and then so that you're sure your opponent can't ignore it. Be understanding and be patient. If the details and ramifications of the deal are complex, don't present them all at once. Offer them slowly and gradually, so that the other side has a chance to assimilate each one before being hit with another.

Basic Psychology

Make your points in a nonthreatening way by asking questions and soliciting advice.

When you want to challenge someone, don't say, "Why didn't you do A?" Instead, say, "Did you think of doing B?" or "What would have happened had you done C?" Questions can be used aggressively. But they can also be used positively, to lead the conversation along a particular path and to achieve a mutually agreeable settlement. If you know where you want to go, begin by asking the other side's advice about what *they* would do. Then use leading questions, like "Wouldn't it be possible to . . ." and "Isn't it true that . . ." to direct the answers toward your goal. This way you will involve your opponent in the solution, and may even persuade him it was his idea in the first place!

Use your opponent's objections to support your own position.

You've made your offer. Now your opponent objects to it: too little, too cumbersome, too one-sided, he says. What you do is ask him to expand on his criticism of your proposal and tell you what's wrong with it. As he speaks, listen carefully. Maybe he's got a point. Maybe he's just objecting for the sake of being disagreeable. Keep a mental list of all he says. After he's done, tell him that you understand his objections and, in fact, have already considered them in your planning. Use each objection as a springboard to present a positive aspect of the proposal you are making. By structuring your argument to mirror your opponent's objections, you are essentially giving your opponent exactly the settlement he is looking for.

Lower your opponent's level of expectations by a judicious choice of words and gestures.

If your opponent believes he's not going to get any more out of you, he'll stop asking. Never let on what you're really willing to accept. Instead, when the other side makes their first offer, make a face of mild disappointment. Introduce information about other offers you have had (and turned down) or about all the positive plans you have made in the event negotiations don't work out. Even if your opponent suspects you're bluffing, it's best to make him wonder, even just a little. That way, he'll be less likely to try to push you over the threshold. This is a good technique to use when you suspect you have the inferior position. COROLLARY: Don't volunteer an "acceptable range" of offers. Your opponent will never offer you more than the lowest you have said you will take.

Put silence to work as a strategic tool.

American negotiators often blow it in Japan by reacting, with embarrassment and nervous prattle, to what for the Japanese is a perfectly natural silence. You don't have to be Japanese to use *not* speaking to your advantage. (1) Silence often prompts the other side to speak, and may result in their revealing useful information. (2) Silence creates the impression of confidence in your position, which may cause your opponent to make concessions. (3) Silence breaks the rhythm of negotiations and allows for a strategic parry. (4) Silence gives your opponent free rein to think the worst. TURNABOUT: If your opponent gives *you* the silent treatment, look calm and keep still—if you do decide to speak, stray from the previous topic.

Basic Psychology

Get your opponent to participate in the decision-making process to insure he'll support the decision.

Even when the deck is stacked in your favor, if you simply impose your decision on your opponent you will likely meet resentment and only halfhearted acceptance of the agreement. Your best bet is to involve him in the chain of reasoning that leads to the decision, so that he feels he is a part of it and that the decision is, to an extent, inevitable. This tactic is especially useful when confronting an employee whose performance has been unsatisfactory; the employee can end up giving himself the option of either straightening out or resigning. Either way, he's bound to feel less resentful. EXAMPLE: A company suffering from wrongful firing suits began using employee review panels with the employee present. Turnover dropped *and* productivity increased.

Never let your opponent know what a good deal you got.

Bragging about how you bested someone in an important negotiation is a sign of insecurity. It's also not very smart. Many settlements involve continuing follow-ups, so the person you "beat" may very well be someone you'll have to deal with again and again. If word gets back and he feels you're talking about him and making him appear stupid or inexperienced in front of other people, he is going to become unhappy and hostile. Gloating after the deal is also exceedingly bad manners. The best advice: keep your boasting and pride to yourself, where it can't hurt you or anybody else.

Basic Psychology

Overwinning can ultimately collapse the deal.

Suppose your opponent blunders and is about to give away the store. Or you've got him pinned to the ground, and you both know it. What should you do? You should first ask yourself whether you want to make an enemy out of this person. Anyone so badly beaten is going to come looking for revenge. Maybe not tomorrow. But someday. He may renege on the deal. He may poison the well. He may even come swooping back as your fiercest competitor. If you're about to get everything you want and then some, go on, give a little back in return for good relations and security. TECHNIQUE: If you're going to be magnanimous, at least put it to your advantage and make sure it's noticed. Go for broke, and then relent "in the interest of goodwill."

Make it easy for your opponent to save face when he backs down or gives concessions.

Sometimes your opponent will want to settle but won't because it'll look like he's caving in. Or sometimes he may really be caving in and is getting angry because you've got him over a barrel. Always make your opponent feel that the deal is the best one he could have gotten. Put a good spin on the result. Ask him to handle the public announcement. If you've just denied a salary increase (and called your employee's bluff that he would quit, knowing that he wouldn't), throw in a little something—a bonus, personal praise—to soften the blow.

Make sure your opponent feels good at the close of negotiations—if you ever hope to deal with him again.

Any negotiation that ends in bitterness or regret is a bad deal whose consequences will come back to haunt you later. If you're developing a relationship with a supplier, don't think of your first deal as a way of showing who's boss. Aim for fairness and take a long-term view of your relationship. If you start out too one-sided, before you know it you'll be looking for a new supplier all over again. Treat your opponent with honor. If you've knocked him down, pick him up. A telephone call the next day, a thank-you note, an invitation to dinner, or a gracious remark to a mutual acquaintance are all ways of making your opponent feel that, if he had to lose, at least he lost to a decent guy.

CHAPTER 3

Short Negotiations

If you're only going to negotiate with your opponent once, it doesn't matter what he thinks of you.

You don't want to strain your relationship with your opponent if you're going to be dealing with him again in the future. But if this is the one and only time, you can be as pushy, tough, and crazy as you like. The best place for the "one and only" method is your local stereo shop or car dealership, where the sales personnel themselves depend upon aggression and intimidation. ERROR: Just because you can act obnoxious and get away with it is no reason to do it. You may not feel good if you've forced yourself to act out of character just to save a couple bucks. On the other hand, it might be worth finding out how it feels to act tough—you might discover you're better at it than you realized, and that it gets real results.

In quick and simple negotiations, forget about strategy. Simply ask for what you want.

Why use elaborate strategies when the issues are basically straightforward? Sometimes the quickest way to get what you want is to ask for it. If the other side says yes ("Sure I can take ten percent off") then the matter is settled. If the answer is no, you may have a better idea of exactly what negotiating tack to take in order to get your way. TIP: Don't begin your negotiations with long-winded rationalizations about your needs. State your objective clearly at the beginning to disarm your opponent and to make sure he doesn't get distracted with wondering what you're getting at.

Just because your opponent has a "firm" policy doesn't mean the policy can't be changed.

When the sales person or personnel supervisor invokes the magic words "that's not our policy," we tend to hear it as a message from on high. Or when we're shown a purchase contract with all the clauses neatly typeset in authoritarian lawyer language, we accept it without question. Don't forget: behind every word and every "policy" is a human being. Policies are often written down for convenience, not intimidation. And they *can* be changed, if not by a lowly clerk, then by a supervisor or store owner. Question authority, and don't accept everything you read.

Use any excuse to ask for a price reduction.

You don't always have to pay sticker price. Many stores will give you a break on demonstration models, on items that have been returned, and on goods with minor defects. It doesn't hurt to ask. Also, be creative. How can you save the store money, and if you save them money why not split the difference? If delivery is included, say you'll haul it away yourself. Bunch your purchases and demand a volume discount. Maybe you can barter a service, like advertising, painting, or printing. In the absence of any good excuse, you can always put your foot down and refuse to buy unless you get a better deal. EXAMPLE: Bill, who lived only a half mile from the department store's warehouse, got the normal mattress delivery charge of $35 reduced to $10 because of the amount of time he was saving the truck driver.

Titillate your opponent into wanting what you have to offer.

Why does the car salesman always wait until after you've touched the new car and gone for a test drive to start talking about price? Because he knows that the desire for the car he's created in you has softened you up. He's converted part of you into his best ally—and now you have to fight him *and* yourself. To create desire in your opponent, appeal not to reason but to lust, greed, and ambition—without using those words. Instead, use flattery, the promise of a corner office, hints of greater rewards to come, and a sprinkling of power jargon. Give your opponent a reason to be unreasonable.

Generate a competitive demand for whatever you have.

Let it be known that you have other options to choose from and that you don't have to make a deal today. Competition works in several ways. (1) If someone else wants what you have, it must be good. (2) The fear is, "If I don't buy it, someone else will." (3) The threat of competition speeds negotiations and narrows the bargaining range. Use the competitive threat judiciously, since your opponent may very well call your bluff. Sometimes it pays to shop around for a competitive, albeit less attractive, option simply to have it in your arsenal. TIMING: The time to ask for a raise is when you have job offers from two other companies. SLEIGHT OF HAND: At the negotiating table, "accidentally" open your file to reveal the business card of your opponent's chief competitor.

Offer extra premiums to make your proposal seem more attractive.

Is there anything about the deal that means more to your opponent than it does to you, something that you could give up and not miss at all? If so, hold this item—be it a concession or an actual object—back from the deal until late in the game. If the buyer won't meet your price, throw in that washing machine (too big and expensive to move anyway) to clinch the sale. PREPARATION: Before the negotiation, make a list of all the possible premiums and, based on your research, decide which ones your opponent cares about most. Release these premiums slowly, one at a time, and watch your opponent to see if they're having the desired effect.

Make your opponent feel you are an expert, and he will respect you more.

The shopping-mall optician is just another clerk. But with his white medical jacket he wears the mantle of authority and knowledge. In a negotiation, you should pay attention to how you "dress" too. If your opponent perceives you as an expert, as a technical whiz, or as someone who knows the secret background behind the offer, he will be less likely to try to fool you or be unreasonable. Play up your experience. Be specific with details. Demonstrate your mastery of the material. And if you lack mastery, bring along an expert to assist you. CAUTION: Watch out for the opponent who tries to test your knowledge with offhand comments. If you are truly ignorant, don't try to play it too smart.

Give your opponent easy decisions to make.

If your offer has a lot of contingencies and qualifications, so will your opponent's response—and you won't really have an agreement. Try to boil down your offer to simple terms so that the other side can either accept or reject them. In a complex negotiation, move ahead one item at a time—yes or no? Structuring the offer like this demands clear thinking and good organization. Write each point you need to cover on a separate card. When you can't simplify, present the other side with several options, and ask them to choose which one they like best. In this way you can build a settlement from the ground up, with both of you participating and choosing.

Short Negotiations

When the negotiation is just about concluded, you can usually extract one more concession.

No one is going to let a major fish get away because he doesn't want to use an extra worm as bait. When the deal is really close make one last demand. This can't be a substantive demand, one that would change the whole shape of the deal—that would only make your opponent angry. Instead, ask for a minor concession, something to sweeten the pot. Like a toolkit for the car, or a box of computer paper to go with your new printer. You'll find most salesmen, driven as they are by the lust for settlement, will quickly cave in if the concession is small enough and if it's late enough in the game.

It's often better to negotiate the price of the product *after* you've used it.

You'd be surprised at the number of people who render services without discussing the price beforehand. The home handyman is a good example. He may come up with a rough materials cost or hourly estimate before he starts. But this is not the same as a firm bid. After he's done the work you have more negotiating room, because he's not in a position to walk away and may take less than he would have agreed to earlier. Similarly, if you have any doubt about whether a store will accept your check or I.D., ask them *after* they've rung up the sale and have to choose between taking your word or crediting the cash register and restocking the shelves.

Make your opponent invest time in you so he's more likely to make concessions to close the deal.

Don't just walk into a store and start negotiating a deal on the washing machine with the salesman. Make him expend time and energy on you first. The easiest way is to ask questions, lots of them. Ask about other, competing models and how they differ from the one he's showing you. Have him explain store policies and aftercare, including warranties and maintenance. Take your time. Then leave the store and go back the next day and ask the same person for more help. By doing this you're getting your opponent to invest his time, and thus increase his stake in the settlement. If you walk away emptyhanded he'll get nothing for his efforts. Become your opponent's "bird in the hand."

Never negotiate on the telephone unless you initiate the call and are totally prepared to talk details.

Whoever makes the phone call has the advantage in a negotiation. The caller chooses a time and a medium (the telephone) that's good for *him*. He's prepared and has his notes at the ready, and he's been thinking about what he's going to say. If your landlord phones you to talk about a rent hike, put him off until you've had a chance to arm yourself and consider your options (What repairs are needed? Does the Fire Department know about the code violations? Will I threaten to move out?). TACTIC: Say this when you're caught unprepared: "Sorry. I can't talk right now. What's a good time I can call you back tomorrow?"

Use the telephone for short and sweet negotiations, and when you have the stronger arguments.

Compared to face-to-face negotiations, telephone negotiations are shorter, more competitive, and more formal. You discuss the matter at hand and don't get sidetracked by pleasantries. Unable to see the other side's reaction, you press your point harder. So, if you're a tough guy, the phone is for you. And if your side is looking at the numbers, while the other side is appealing to the heart, insist on talking over the phone. In a tightly structured situation like a phone conversation, clear, rational arguments gain extra strength.

Always have a ready answer to your opponent's questions—even if it's only a reworking of something you just said.

The worst thing that can happen is when your opponent asks you a question and you just sit there at a loss for words. Even if you recover, your opponent will perceive a weakness, and he won't let go of it without inflicting injury. Your best defense is to anticipate the questions you'll be asked. Why is the price so high? Why can't I get the goods in three months? What happened to the collateral? When taken by surprise, turn the question into one you've answered previously. Take it back to the issue of price, for example, or, without committing to specifics, restate your willingness to be reasonable. OBSERVE: Watch politicians on the Sunday morning TV interview shows. They are masters of the deft answer. Notice they never address the exact question but return to their stump speech on the subject.

After a telephone negotiation, write a memo of the terms discussed and send it to your opponent.

Most people think a follow-up memo to a phone call is merely a paper record of what was talked about. That's wrong—a memo you send an opponent is an important negotiating tool. It concretizes the agreement, and offers you the opportunity to further refine your position. That's why you should write it, and not your opponent. If a point was left vague in the conversation, you can either clarify it or omit it. Also, since subsequent discussions will focus on the memo and not the conversation that preceded it, the memo gives you control over the content and limits of the final agreement. DEFENSE: When your opponent suggests that *he* prepare the memo, you suggest that both of you do it and compare notes.

CHAPTER 4

Longer Negotiations

If you regularly negotiate with the same opponent, periodically change your negotiating style.

If your usual opponent has you psyched out, if he knows how you think and what you're looking for, he has a tremendous advantage and can easily manipulate you. Don't give him the chance. Be inconsistent. Vary your approach. Be accommodating one day, demanding the next. Insist on changing the venue of the session, from an office to a restaurant. Make an unexpected concession—agree, for example, to pay the first price asked and don't even try to beat your opponent down. By refusing to let your opponent use your own psychology against you, you force him to stick to the issues and to approach you with more caution and respect.

Begin protracted negotiations with a statement expressing a desire for a solution of mutual benefit.

Many negotiations begin—and end unsuccessfully—with the principals thinking only of what they are going to get out of the settlement. The basic negotiating maxim is that each side must feel the terms are beneficial to them or they won't go along with it. That being the case, why not put this point paramount in everyone's mind at the outset? Do just that. In your opening statement emphasize that your ultimate goal is to fashion an agreement of mutual benefit to both sides. List the interests you have in common, such as collateral and security, orderly transfer of power, survival of the organization, and so on. When you hit a snag, go back to basics and re-examine the issue in the light of the principle of mutual benefit.

Treat your opponent with consideration and generosity, even as you attack his position with vigor and toughness.

It's tempting sometimes to give in on an important point just to be accommodating. Don't get confused about why you're negotiating. You're there to gain a settlement, not to win a popularity contest. It's just as tempting, however, to be overtly hostile to your opponent so as not to appear weak. Smart negotiators learn to distinguish between the people they're negotiating with and the problem they're negotiating about. Being nice to the other side increases the likelihood that they'll be swayed by the facts supporting your position.

If your opponent is a lot stronger than you, structure the negotiation around facts, figures, and accepted precedent.

When you lack power, use knowledge and hard numbers to reach a settlement. A large organization can bully you, and maybe even bring in experts to talk rings around you. But if you know your car or your job is worth a certain amount on the market and can back up your contention with facts and figures, you stand a good chance of getting your way. Using objective criteria also helps defuse tension—people don't have to argue with their emotions or their egos but can justify their decisions on neutral grounds. Agreeing to play only by the numbers is a good way to start any negotiation that is traditionally open to intense haggling, like buying a rug or buying a home.

Secretly planting information that will get back to your opponent can lend added strength to your position.

Use tabloid psychology. People may not believe you, but they'll probably believe what other people say about you. Identify the people in your company who are blabbermouths and use them as a means of spreading rumors. Tell them you've been offered another job or are thinking of quitting. Then go to the boss and pitch for a higher salary.

If your opponent brings in an expert, bring in a more "expert" expert.

Don't be intimidated by the fancy professionals your opponent brings in to dazzle you with their knowledge and befuddle you with their jargon. Be skeptical, but polite. The next day, go in with your own expert, someone with even better credentials who can play the same game back. As in a court of law, the expert witness represents credibility and established authority. But use your expert carefully—coach him in all the issues under discussion and make sure he understands what the point is you want him to make. CAUTION: Never let the expert take over the discussion. By having him defer to you, you establish your own authority as well.

Use people in your opponent's network to influence him.

Few decision makers operate totally in a vacuum. They rely on those around them to provide information, analysis, and advice. Your strategy should be to make sure your opponent's support staff is favorably disposed to your proposition. Use industry gatherings and conferences to meet these people. Talk to them informally. Make up an excuse to chat over the phone. Present information that benefits you. If possible, discuss your situation with a third party who is a friend or trusted advisor of your adversary, and ask him to give you a personal introduction. Should you receive assistance, *never* forget to express your appreciation. TIP: Often the ones with most influence are the low-level clerks and secretaries who see the boss every day and are in a position to filter the information that reaches him. Be unfailingly courteous and respectful to the "front desk" people.

Try to get your opponent to make the first offer.

You and your opponent dance cautiously around the table. Who's going to make the first offer? Not you! The other side may be feeling cautious or generous—or maybe their accountant goofed. Let them go first, and you can then feel out their position. Even if the deal they offer isn't quite right, at least you know roughly what they're thinking and whether you're in for a real uphill battle. Of course your opponent approaches the table with the same strategy to use against you. Generally the one who's selling can be persuaded to name his price, on the grounds that he knows the numbers and the circumstances of the sale.

Tell your opponent about the obvious weaknesses in your position before he tells you.

Many states require that you fully disclose the condition of your home when you put it up for sale. This is for the protection of the buyer, of course, but notice how easy it makes one aspect of the negotiation—the buyer no longer has to quibble about the quality of the goods, because it is already reflected in the asking price. If you're selling a figurine or piece of furniture with obvious (and even not so obvious) damage, point it out to the purchaser. Because you're being honest, it's more likely the buyer will perceive the price you're asking as a fair one.

Find out your opponent's deadline, but don't let him know yours.

Whether you're selling a house, heading off a strike, or trying to generate cash before the note comes due, settlement deadlines concentrate the mind wonderfully. As the deadline nears, your opponent grows more anxious, and he may be inclined to make large concessions that he wouldn't have made earlier on. Therefore, don't settle too soon into the session unless you have to—things may improve for you down the line. Keep your own time agenda hidden. Be casual about the time. Say that you're willing to go past the deadline to get a settlement, and observe the other side's reaction. CAUTION: Deadlines can sometimes drive the parties to act tough and turn on the pressure. Beware of the "deadline" that is simply a ploy to draw you into an agreement.

Purposely delay the negotiations to test your opponent's need to settle.

When scheduling a negotiation, don't appear eager to begin. Rather, suggest that the negotiations be put off because (1) you're too busy, (2) you've got an important conference to prepare for, (3) you're just looking around and aren't ready to decide—this last is a good ploy to use in an electronics store. Your opponent, if he's desperate for the deal, may try to speed the process by immediately making you a good offer. Even when he agrees to your delay, if he calls you back in a week or so to ask if you're ready, you'll know that for whatever reason he wants to make a deal and that you can probably push harder and farther than you had originally thought possible.

Try to conduct negotiations at times when you are not desperately dependent on a favorable outcome.

It's one thing to talk price when you're putting the seed in the ground, and quite another when your crop is harvested. The farmer with a truckload of vegetables *has* to sell, or he'll lose everything, and will likely accept a lower price than if he had arranged for the sale earlier. Let this be a lesson to you, too. If you have a pressing deadline or a need for cash, don't wait until the last minute to make your move. Reasons: (1) The deadline will force you to accept an unfavorable settlement. (2) Your anxiety will betray you to your opponent, and may cloud your thinking.

Never negotiate with anyone who has less authority to make concessions than you do.

There's no point in making concessions to the other side if all your opponent does is tell you, at the end of the day, that he must now clear the deal with his superiors. You've already shown your hand, so tomorrow the other side will come back asking for more. If you can't avoid dealing with an unempowered subordinate, (1) be as stingy as you can and (2) tell your opponent that you have the right to rethink the terms too. TURNABOUT: You can use an imaginary "boss" as a ploy of your own, either to defer a commitment or as a means of getting out of a deal that you belatedly realize is not in your best interests.

If your opponent lacks authority, insist that your agreement be approved step by step.

At the car dealership, you talk at length with the salesman, who finally agrees to your demands. He then comes back to tell you "the boss" won't go for it. Lots of deals unravel at the last minute because the top guy, who wasn't present at the negotiations, says no. To prevent this from happening when bargaining with subordinates, divide your proposition into separate pieces. Present each piece as a discrete deal in itself, and insist that it be approved by the boss before you move on to the next item. This "accrual method" locks in your agreement and also has the psychological effect of discouraging your adversary by constantly reminding him of his powerlessness.

Join two issues together when you know the other side definitely wants to give in on one of them.

If an employer offers you a great assignment, and you know he really needs you, don't just say yes off the bat. Use his need for you as leverage to settle secondary issues that might be harder to negotiate later—like the amount of bonus pay, that new company car, or a new job title. Similarly, don't wait until you're about to ink the purchase contract for a new car to bring up talk about an extended warranty. By then you're too committed. Bring up the warranty early on, so that when you're talking price everything's included. The salesperson wants to sell you the car, and if he thinks the deal's contingent on the warranty price he'll make it sweet for you.

Make negotiating concessions sparingly on the basis of a considered response.

Timing and style are supremely important when making concessions. Remember, every concession you make indicates a softening in your position. If you make the hole too big, your opponent will jump into the breach and try to inflict more serious damage. Basic rules: Make your concessions sound justified by circumstances. Never let on that you are acting under pressure. Think about why your opponent wants the concession (does he really need it to make the deal work, or is he just trying to push you around?). Keep your concessions small. Make only one concession at a time.

Never give away something unless you receive something in return.

Every concession you make depreciates the value of your final settlement. You must therefore insist on getting something in return for everything you give away. Simply demonstrating your virtue in the hope it will pay off down the line is not good enough. When your opponent says, "I want you to give me A," you should say, "And what will you give me?" If your opponent doesn't offer anything in return, you (1) know what sort of hardliner you're dealing with and (2) can feel justified in hardening your own position. RESULT: Your opponent will be less likely to come at you with a request again without having something in hand to trade.

Keep your concessions small—but make your opponent think they're big so he'll reciprocate big.

Never give in without a fight, even if what you're losing is of little consequence. In fact, you should always try to give up the things that matter to you least, even while you act as if it really hurts to do so. This increases the value of your concession and makes your opponent feel he must give away something big in return. PLOY: Pump up your opening position with several plausible-sounding items you don't really care about. Give these away first—your opponent may even let you end up keeping some of them.

If you give your opponent an ultimatum, make it mild, and do so only at the end of the negotiation.

It serves no purpose to tell the other side that your offer is their "last chance" if negotiations have barely begun. They're likely to call your bluff and, rightly, look at your threat as a sign of the inherent weakness of your position. Save your ultimatum to the end. When you make it, explain rationally with facts and figures why you have been forced to do so. Offer a choice—"either pay me in cash or in kind"—so that your opponent feels a part of the decision and won't later resist or subvert the settlement. TOO HASTY: The Merrills lost the architect they really wanted for their remodeling by telling him at the start he'd have to lower his fee. They should have waited until he was so interested in the project that he would have worked for less.

Specify exactly what it was you agreed to at the end of a negotiating session.

Never let a negotiation end without both sides agreeing to a summary of the settlement reached. Otherwise, you run the risk of somebody forgetting what was agreed to or, worse, coming back later to renegotiate a point that was supposed to have been worked out. Points to include are: (1) the terms of the settlement, (2) who does what, (3) the time frame, and (4) "what ifs" ("what if I don't get my money in time?") and penalties. If possible, commit the summary to writing. CRUCIAL: If the deal is particularly important or has legal ramifications, you should of course follow up the summary with an actual contract.

CHAPTER 5

More Formal Negotiations: Contracts, Consultants, and Bureaucracies

Even the most official-looking contracts can be altered through negotiation.

Lots of small businesses and freelance professionals use "standard" contracts. These are prepared by their business associations or in many cases by a stationery company for sale in ordinary shops. What's "standard" about these contracts is the way they favor the business owner. Don't be fooled. Just because a contract is printed and sounds legalistic doesn't mean it can't be changed. Ask for offending clauses to be struck out or reworded. Since it *can* be changed, read the contract carefully before signing. Don't listen when the salesman says, "It's just legal stuff; don't worry about it." SAFETY TIP: Always insist that contract alterations be written and initialed by each side. Keep a photocopy of the final, signed contract.

Sensitive issues might be easier to agree on if they are made the subject of a side memo instead of being put in the main contract.

Your opponent may refuse to write something in a formal contract because he does not want his other clients (or the company accountants) to find out about it. For example, a publisher's policy limits an author to fifteen complimentary copies of his book when it is published. But you insist on getting fifty. Rather than write that in the contract, your editor says he will send thirty-five extra promotional copies to anyone you tell him to. You agree, and make a memo to this effect that you can use should he "forget" (or lose his job). Trust is essential in this situation, but your willingness to trust your opponent's word can itself be a kind of concession that you can use to get a better deal.

Don't be intimidated by professionals.

Never let your lack of expertise or the lawyer's or doctor's fancy title prevent you from asking questions and pursuing what you want. It's in the professional's own interest to keep you at arm's length, and to treat you like a helpless child. And it's our own basic nature to trust those in positions of authority. Fight this tendency by writing down everything you need to ask about— especially fees and extra charges. Press your points— show that even though you may not understand the technical points, you do understand business. EXAMPLE: Ed insisted that his tax attorney explain everything to him in plain English with the very convincing threat, "If I can't understand it, I won't sign it and you won't get paid!"

It's perfectly acceptable to negotiate with professionals about their fees before *and* after services are rendered.

Professionals would have you believe it's unseemly to talk about money—but they don't hesitate to charge you for every little paper clip and phone call. If you are considering working with a lawyer, accountant, or even a doctor, talk about the fees early in your initial meeting. If you think they're too expensive, say so, and ask if you can get the price reduced. Perhaps there are things you can do to keep costs down—like typing your own contract drafts. And if the bill you're presented with seems out of line, explain why and ask that it be reduced. Most professionals don't want to stoop to haggling about price either, and if you have good reasons—financial need, bad results—you can probably get them to agree to go along with your proposal.

Sometimes it's wise to retain an agent to negotiate on your behalf.

Hiring a professional—an agent, attorney, or broker —to work for you can be a good idea. He can be hard-nosed where you're not. And if he's an expert, the other side knows they can't outjargon him. Never give your hired gun complete decision-making power. His limited authority works to your advantage, in that he can draw concessions from the other side without being able to make any himself. Give him realistic goals in the negotiation, but also use him to shield your true settle-ment point from view. EXAMPLE: John, the irascible and vindictive surviving partner, resisted paying his de-ceased partner's estate its due for the business. The family members, intimidated by John's attitude, hired a no-holds-barred negotiator to fight for a settlement, and paid him a percentage of what he managed to get over John's original offer.

Lawyers, brokers, and agents work first and foremost for themselves.

When you send your lawyer in to do battle, who is he working for? For himself. In most cases, he does better if you do better, but not always. If you resist a "fair" settlement, you may find your lawyer pressuring you to go against your better judgment, only because he's decided the extra work you're asking him to do will not be adequately compensated in the long run. Or what about your stockbroker? He wants you to do well, but even if you do poorly and sell out your position he still makes money. REMEMBER: Sometimes it's to your benefit to keep secrets from the people you hire—they may work better if they don't know your real financial situation, or that you have other professionals advising you on the side. The point is, never give up total control to anyone.

Work *with* your agent.

An agent can help your career or your negotiation. Don't think, though, that just because you've hired an agent all your business problems are solved. Agents require your cooperation and close supervision: (1) Tell the agent exactly what you want to have done. (2) Explain the Three R's and insist on Reports, Record-keeping, and Results. (3) Provide information and ideas promptly when the agent asks for them. (4) Keep the agent in an advisory function; never let him make important decisions on your behalf. (5) Make sure you and the agent see eye to eye on risk strategies: if you're ready to settle, don't let the agent gamble or bluff your chances away.

Government bureaucracies respond best to those who are vocal about their needs, desires, and dissatisfactions.

Forget all that one-man, one-vote stuff. Government bureaucrats can't be fired and have learned to respond only to those who scream loudest and longest about their particular franchise. Where you as a consumer can make demands on private industry, the irate taxpayer demanding his due is just sneered at by government workers. The only reason they'll do anything to help you is when you persuade them you will make even more work for them if they don't. BEST APPROACH: Come on as helpless, in need of expert assistance, humble before the knowledgeable bureaucrat. But be persistent. Call every day, even while you remain a supplicant.

When dealing with bureaucracies, first find the right person to deal with.

How often have you explained your needs at length over the phone only to be told at the end that you're talking to the wrong department? Don't waste time, and don't risk accessing the bureaucracy through a powerless door. Public records will list the municipal officers. Or call general information and narrow your search from there. If you start out in the wrong place, administrative bungling can hang you up or even damage you. WARNING: Sometimes you will get an eager-beaver, bored-to-tears, low-level bureaucrat who will take up your cause just to give himself something to do. These people are dangerous. Ambitious but in actuality powerless, they can prevent you from reaching the people who can really solve your problem. Always find out a person's official rank before giving him any responsibility.

The closer you get to the top in a bureaucracy, the more likely you'll get satisfactory results.

People at the top of the bureaucratic heap have two qualities you can put to work: (1) they have decision-making power and (2) they don't always feel they have to follow rules and regulations to the letter. Many department heads are in fact extremely well educated, proud of their jobs, and distanced enough from the drudgery and paperwork to have a pleasant, "can do" attitude. They enjoy putting the wheels of government into motion. INSIGHT: Favors and connections count for everything. Ask your colleagues, especially your lawyer, if they know anyone in government who can take you right to the top. Even if his friend is not in the right department for your problem, he will probably know someone who is, and will gladly introduce you to demonstrate his power and influence.

Lower-level employees will readily give out insider information.

Clerks and secretarial staff can tell you how the system *really* works, because they have to use it themselves every day. Types of information they can give you: (1) who's in charge, (2) which rules count and which can be ignored, (3) when is the best time to confront the boss, (4) what is effective and what isn't. Large corporations especially are susceptible to low-level penetration. Pushing and cajoling are good techniques, especially with younger employees. With older workers, it is generally better to approach them with proper deference to their knowledge and experience.

Get people in large institutions and bureaucracies to identify with you as a person.

As much as possible, personalize your contacts with otherwise faceless clerks and administrators. Always give your name. Always get the name of the person you're speaking with. When you call back for follow-up (when making travel arrangements, for example), ask for the person who handled your call previously. Try to put your request in terms that make it distinctive, and that the other person can relate to ("I'm doing this for my father, who's been very ill recently"). It's easy for people to reject you if you're just a number, but once you have a name and a "story" to go with it, you become harder to ignore. If you don't have a story . . . make one up.

When dealing with a bureaucracy, set a time limit for results and monitor the progress of your negotiation.

Always keep records of your calls to a bureaucracy. Write down what was promised. Make sure the clerk gives you an action deadline. Send a letter summarizing your conversation. Call the same clerk back on the day of the deadline. If no action has been taken, ask to speak to a supervisor. Again, get a deadline and follow up with a letter and phone call. If this still doesn't work, move up to the next supervisory level. If you work the system persistently and lay a paper trail, with a record of missed deadlines and failed promises, you will eventually get what you want.

Never let "official policy" be the reason you don't get satisfaction.

If you ever get stonewalled with the words, "That's just not our policy," remember that somewhere in the organization there is a person who has the power to override. Ask to speak to him. If that doesn't work, ask to see exactly how the policy is worded. It may be that no such policy exists, or that your situation could be interpreted as an allowable exception to it. One good technique is to say, "Suppose it was possible to do what I ask, how would you go about it?" INSIGHT: Once you've made the clerk explain how the system might work for you, he'll have less resistance to making it actually happen.

Figure out which office or agency to threaten to contact if satisfaction isn't forthcoming.

Threatening specific action is very effective. When arguing with a merchant, for example, mention the Better Business Bureau or your credit card company. Name the merchant's or manufacturer's association (and what city it's in). Threaten to call your local talk radio consumer affairs program. When dealing with government offices, dangle the name of the applicable government regulatory agency, or the name of your elected representative. Your opponent doesn't want publicity or hassles. Your job is to make him realize that it is going to be cheaper and more painless to give you what you want.

Never negotiate in the name of an institution. Instead, negotiate for yourself as a human surrogate *for* the institution.

People don't want to do things for your company. They want to do things for *you*. Try to get your opponent to see through your official role to the person within you. Even though you may be there on behalf of your government or corporation, you will get good results to the extent you can show human feelings and make the other side feel they are dealing with a reasonable and compassionate person. When negotiating a charitable contribution, speak from your experience so that the other side feels there's a legitimacy to your request. EXCEPTION: If the company or institution you're representing is big and powerful, invoking its name may generate fear and awe—but do so only if fear and awe are what you need to reach a settlement.

CHAPTER 6

What to Do at an Impasse

Don't be put off by the word "no."

The word "no" in a negotiation is usually code for "not right now," or "not exactly," or "maybe, but I'm not going to give in just now." Take similar negative absolutes—like "impossible," "never," "no way"—as invitations to keep talking. After all, if your opponent really thought a deal was out of the question he would get up and leave the room. GAMBIT: When you meet a stone wall of negativity, turn the situation around. Ask your opponent directly, "What would it take to get you to say yes?"

Skip over the points that are bogging you down and come back to them later.

You may find you and your opponent thrashing around a certain point without reaching any agreement, or even coming close. Rather than jeopardize the entire negotiation, suggest that the sticking point be put aside for now and returned to after other matters have been settled. By looking at other parts of the negotiation, you may discover a way through the impasse. Also, if you and your opponent can find yourself working together harmoniously elsewhere, you may find it easier to carry that same spirit over to the point of real contention. Whatever you do, don't take trouble at one point as an indication that the entire negotiation is doomed.

When deadlocked, get back to common ground and start building up again.

One good trick for dealing with a deadlock in your negotiations is to stop arguing details and verbally summarize all the points you have in common. Mention all the things you've agreed on up to now, and emphasize your common goals. Then take your deadlock issue and try to frame it in terms of these common goals. Analyze exactly what it is that's preventing you from coming to an agreement. Maybe it's money, yes, but money how? What does your opponent need that money for—to buy another company? To retire? Perhaps you can address that hidden agenda more directly. In any case, by "agreeing" on the cause of the deadlock and on your common desire for a settlement, you can often use the momentum of harmony to break through the impasse.

Break down complex negotiations into pieces, and solve each piece one at a time.

Keep the big picture in mind, but don't get lost in it. Complex negotiations can often be helped by fragmentation. For example, don't just think in large terms about "buying the house." Instead, look at all the aspects of the purchase and take them up one at a time with the agent: title, broker's commission, pest report, furnishings, selling price. Keep a list and check each item off as you go. You will find they all relate to each other, of course, but by discussing them individually you can reach agreement on particular points as you gradually work up to the main settlement. TIP: In very complex negotiations, how you choose to fragment the issues is extremely important. Group issues (1) according to ease of settlement or (2) according to "discomfort" level, so that you can pace the discussions by mixing equal doses of harmony and confrontation.

Brainstorm with your opponent to generate different options.

There are times when the best approach is to drop your guard and just think out loud about possible solutions. Tell your opponent that you are going "off the record" and are not offering up your ideas as formal proposals. Rather, suggest that by just kicking ideas around together perhaps you can find one that will work for both of you. This is a classic "good faith" gambit, because you have to trust your opponent won't use your ideas against you later. Let brainstorming rules apply: Voice any idea, no matter how impractical. Don't react positively or negatively, but just get the idea on the table. Always offer more than one idea at a time to make sure you're not creatively blocking yourself in.

Fine tune your agreement so that there is *something* that both you and your opponent find acceptable.

Remember that you and your opponent are going to see your final agreement in very different ways. You're buying a house and paying for it over time. He's selling a house—maybe he wants the money now, maybe he wants it later, and depending on which it is he will adjust the asking price. Use this idea in reverse. If you can't agree on price, agree on payment terms instead, and let that determine the price. Or, agree to a limited-term agreement instead of a permanent one. Or, go for an exclusive right instead of a nonexclusive one. Look beyond the bottom line, take out your wrench, and start tinkering.

Passing proposal drafts back and forth for criticism and response builds consensus painlessly.

Say you and a friend are buying a house together and can't agree on terms. Instead of both of you trying to work out all the details in conversation, take the initiative by actually drafting a model agreement. Then show the agreement to your partner and ask him to note all the areas where he is in disagreement or that he feels are missing. He then passes the revised draft back to you, and now it's your turn to make revisions and comments. You'll probably have to go through several such drafts to reach a final agreement. But by the process of revising a little bit each time you will avoid bloodshed and produce a contract you and your friend can both live with.

When things aren't going your way, call for a time out.

Never let the negotiation run away from you. If you're feeling pressured, tired, or on the verge of defeat, call a break, even if you have to make up an excuse on the spot (bathroom trips are good for brief interludes). Use the break to relax and think about how to handle the discussion. Get your emotions under control. Sometimes a short break is all that's needed to diffuse the tension in the room. But if things are really bad, say that you need time to think and collect new data and suggest returning to the table tomorrow. NOTE: This ploy must be used judiciously, as it undermines your strength and authority. If you anticipate difficult negotiations, schedule them for later in the day to provide you with a natural stopping point at dinnertime.

If you're negotiating with two opponents at a time, try to separate them. Convince the more flexible one, and then both of you convince the hardliner.

Use disagreements among the team you're negotiating against as a wedge to drive them apart. If you can get one of the opposing team in your corner, then the one who remains not only has to fight you but also pressure from within his own organization. A younger negotiator, for example, might be more inclined to move into a risky venture than his conservative boss, and you can use his ambition as a fulcrum to tilt the discussion in your favor. If you're a realtor, get either the husband or wife alone, depending on which seems more interested in the purchase.

Trick a reluctant opponent into negotiating.

Here are some things to do if your opponent outright refuses to even talk to you: (1) Send a letter which outlines your position, and invite him to reply by letter as well. This opens an informal dialogue. (2) Invite one of your opponent's trusted friends or associates to lunch and ask for his assistance. (3) Begin taking actions as if you intend to proceed with or without your opponent's cooperation—send in people to "inspect" the building for renovation, for example—and make sure he hears about it. (4) Be a pest. This is useful for promotion and pay-raise seekers faced with a reluctant boss. Call every day. Attack your opponent outside the elevator. Send flowers (a tactic for couples only).

Your threats will be taken more seriously if you show you intend to carry them out.

Threats are a legitimate tactic, but if your opponent believes you lack the means, guts, or intention to carry a threat out he may call your bluff. So be prepared. First, don't threaten to do the impossible. Second, when you make the threat, pull out supporting documentation —a letter to the newspaper, a purchase order from another company, a copy of the Rent Board's guidelines. EXAMPLE: Faced with a reluctant contractor, Geraldine showed him a copy of the building code, with the phone number of the housing authority underlined in red. TRAP: Too many threats may make the other side feel cornered and respond with a threat of their own.

What to Do at an Impasse

A well-timed emotional outburst can sometimes get your opponent to agree to your terms quickly.

Many issues are not decided rationally at all. Whoever wins is often the one who feels most strongly. When it comes down to that, your best option may be to scream, cry, or become otherwise unreasonable. You may find that the other side doesn't care enough to press the point, or is scared to. Either way, you get what you want without having to justify yourself (thus diverting attention from those areas that wouldn't stand a close inspection). WATCH OUT: Like other gonzo tactics, this one has to be used sparingly, unless you think you can consistently use your reputation as a high-strung hysteric to your advantage.

Try using traditional "fair play" procedures to resolve problems, especially when dealing with family and friends.

"Eeny, meeny, miney, moh" may sound like a kid's game, but it is one of the fairest and most efficient decision-making methods ever devised. When there are lots of claimants and lots of issues, look to formal, arbitrary methods rather than get involved in lengthy and complex negotiations. Other methods: drawing straws, flipping a coin, "stone, scissors, paper," taking turns, football-draft-style selections (the person who got the worst pick on the last round goes first next time, and vice versa), round-robins, and so on. Everyone may end up with a very different amount, but at least no one will complain that the process was unfair.

Appeal to your opponent's ethics and morality.

The sense of fairness underlies most negotiations, and it is good practice to bring it out into the open as a subtle pressure tactic, as in "If I give you this, *it's only fair* that I get something in return." This tactic can be used not only before making your offer but after, as a means of breaking an impasse. Fairness also derives from precedent, and if you can demonstrate that historically your solution has legitimacy your opponent will be less likely to dismiss it out of hand: if it was good enough for Jones, why isn't it good enough for Smith?

Submit your negotiation obstacle to mediation or arbitration.

Procedures for dispute resolution are very well developed in the corporate world, and you can use them as well. If you and your opponent are at a total impasse, first find someone who will mediate your dispute. The mediator will talk to both sides separately and then suggest a solution, which you and your opponent are free to accept or reject. If this doesn't work, you can submit to binding arbitration, and even have the decision of the arbitrator recorded as a legal judgment. These solutions are effective and cost much less than courtroom battles. WHEN TO RESIST: If you clearly hold the upper hand, don't submit to binding arbitration, since you will inevitably be forced to back off your demands.

What to Do at an Impasse

When all else fails, throw yourself on your opponent's mercy.

In a tough situation, make an emotional appeal to your opponent's sense of decency and fair play. If you have special needs—a cash crunch, a deadline, an illness— and if you judge your opponent to be not lacking in compassion, make your situation known and appeal for his consideration. Your opponent, having had the satisfaction of seeing you admit defeat and lie prostrate at his feet, may spare your life to impress you further with his magnanimity. If you're going to get beaten anyway, you may as well try one last act of desperation.

CHAPTER 7

Dirty Tactics and Strategies

Unless you have a good reason to trust your opponent, don't.

Be cautious at all times. You can be certain that your opponent is not going to tell you anything to his disadvantage ("the car's frame was bent in an accident"), and you should assume that he is probably stretching the truth ("runs like new"). The basic negotiating rule is, if you can't verify, don't believe it. Ask for documentation. Become an expert yourself, and check your answers against your opponent's. People will try to make you feel bad for impugning their honesty, for wasting their time. Don't be a sucker. Get everything in writing. If you can't check out all the facts, delay the negotiations or get out of them completely.

If your opponent tries to use a dirty tactic, bring it out in the open and discuss it.

When you spot a tricky deal or shady maneuver, call attention to it. Once the dirty tactic is exposed, it's lost its effectiveness, and you can then use your opponent's lack of good faith against him. Your opponent may retreat, or he may hang tough. What should you do? (1) Don't attack him personally; that only creates defensive aggression. (2) Offer to "forget" the incident and suggest moving on to more productive talks. (3) Walk out and wait for your opponent to call you, or call back in a few days and ask whether he's now ready to proceed in good faith. VARIATION: Don't expose your opponent's tactic at first, but hold it in reserve until you can milk it for maximum benefit ("By the way, what you tried earlier is a bait and switch, and I'll report you if you don't knock another $150 off the price").

Beware of an environment set up to intimidate you.

How you feel affects how you negotiate. In an unfamiliar setting (your opponent's office) surrounded by
unfamiliar people (his staff) you can feel intimidated,
vulnerable, and weakened. Be aware of moods and
atmospheres that can subtly manipulate you. Watch out
especially when food is brought in. Too much food can
make you sleepy—if you must eat, choose light salads.
Never drink alcohol. And watch out especially for
coffee and tea—the tendency is to drink cup after cup,
and this can frazzle your nerves by the end of the day,
just when you have to be most sharp.

Beware of the limited agenda ploy.

Sometimes your opponent will try to restrict the subject
of a negotiation to a single issue. Maybe the boss says
he's only going to discuss working conditions, and not
pay or vacations. Think about why he's doing this—is
he vulnerable on those other points? By controlling the
scope of negotiations, he is controlling the outcome. If
you cede control here you are giving up valuable power.
Offer instead to keep issues separate, but insist that your
main concern be addressed *first*, and then you can go on
to his.

Beware of your opponent's attempt to stall the negotiations.

Your opponent may try to put off your talks or a settlement if he feels there's something to gain by waiting—more pressure on you, lower interest rates, the possibility of better options emerging. When confronted by delaying tactics, try to find real-world incentives for pushing ahead. Examples might be a foreclosure date, a sales conference, the end of the fiscal year, an impending trip abroad. By resorting to outside, immutable conditions, you create a sense of urgency that your opponent will have trouble ignoring. INSIGHT: Your opponent's tactics may in fact be a case of prepartum blues—the unwillingness to surrender a favorite job or possession. Real-world incentives may afford your opponent a welcome means of coming to grips with reality.

Beware of your opponent's assurances that everything will be all right.

Watch out when your opponent says, "Don't worry, you can afford it." His ploy is to keep you talking and to hold off on the bad news until you're farther into the deal. Here are a few countertactics: (1) Use your opponent's vagueness on an issue to build an assumption in your favor into the deal, and tell him that's what you're doing. (2) Start pushing for "guarantee" concessions, such as payment up front and penalty clauses. (3) Keep bringing up the issue to force your opponent to repeat his assurance, so that your position hardens while his grows more defensive.

Beware of your opponent's extreme demands.

Negotiators often assume that settlement will be at a point midway between the two sides' initial offers. Your opponent may try to exploit this assumption by making his initial offer ridiculously high (or low). Don't for a second give this offer any serious consideration, unless you counter with your own ridiculous offer at the other extreme. Instead, demand that your opponent talk in good faith, and threaten to walk away from the table if he doesn't. Less confrontationally, you can also indicate that you know your opponent's demand is absurd, and challenge him to justify it with facts and figures. Of course he won't be able to, and you have effectively destroyed his credibility, something you might be able to put to your advantage later in the talks.

Beware of your opponent's escalating demands.

You extract a concession, but your opponent raises his demand on a separate, settled issue. Or the entire deal is agreed to, and then your opponent comes back and asks to renegotiate one or two points again. It's hard to deal with this reverse-Jello kind of opponent—with him your hard deal has a way of softening. It may be best to simply walk out and refuse to come back until he agrees to adhere to principles—a deal is a deal. But if circumstances have changed for you, too, or if you think there's something you wouldn't mind discussing again, it's perfectly OK to go back to the table. Bear in mind, though, that once a single fissure appears, the whole mountain may open up—sometimes it's best to stick with what you've got.

Beware of opponents who play a zone defense.

You've sparred and made a deal with one opponent when suddenly, as negotiations move along, a new guy is sent in to pick up where the other left off. Now you find yourself being asked for another concession, another percent off. As you move down court, yet another defender picks you up. Don't let this happen to you— refuse to bargain, or be very stingy, as soon as you discover that you keep dealing with different faces and are getting no closer to a settlement. CULTURAL NOTE: The Japanese variation on this is to keep sending in fresh troops to do battle. The afternoon crew (there's always more than one person at a Japanese session) is different from the morning crew. Solution? Get plenty of rest and, if possible, take along a colleague.

Beware of the low-ball gambit.

This is the classic car salesman's routine. He offers you a fantastic price, almost meaning a loss to him. You stop looking elsewhere. Then the salesman starts loading in the extras, or even claiming that the first price he offered you was a "mistake" or that his boss "didn't go for it." Protect yourself: (1) Be suspicious of any deal that seems too good to be true. (2) Get the offer in writing as soon as it's made. (3) If your opponent won't honor his original offer, demand a concession that you didn't get the first time. (4) Appealing to a sleazeball's sense of honor may not work, but it's worth a try, particularly if you can demonstrate your own good faith and the hardship you will suffer if the deal changes. TURNABOUT: Say your boss only grudgingly approved the first deal you struck, and that he won't go for a new one.

Beware of the high-ball gambit.

You've got something to sell. A buyer offers you such a good price you stop taking bids. Then the buyer starts finding reasons to pay you less than he said he would. It's hard to protect yourself, but here are a few things you can do: (1) Don't let greed cloud your thinking. You know about what the deal's worth. If someone goes way beyond that, be suspicious. (2) Remember the deal isn't a deal until the papers are signed. Never close down other options. Keep other offers in reserve. (3) If you do detect bad-faith bargaining, walk away quickly to minimize the damage.

Beware the good cop/bad cop routine.

The classic gambit. You're negotiating with two people, one of whom wants to make the deal with you, while the other refuses. The good cop (now "your friend") asks you to bend a bit to bring the bad cop around. One way of dealing with this is to expose the fiction and thus its power to manipulate you. Say, "Nice routine guys, but let's talk about real issues." Or, you could play along with the gambit and really try to work the good cop against his buddy. Whatever you do, don't forget who's on your side and who's working against you. Resist your tendency to be a diplomat and a nice guy. WATCH OUT: Sometimes the bad cop in the scenario is behind the scenes. He may be a complete fiction. If reference is made to "Mr. Big," ask to meet and talk to him directly.

Beware of verbal and nonverbal personal attacks.

Your opponent may be ill-mannered, or he may be deliberately insulting to rattle and intimidate you. He may abuse you verbally ("That's a stupid idea") or he may be more subtle (like keeping you waiting or chatting on the phone while you're there). Here are two ways to fight back: (1) Simply keep your cool and doggedly persist in getting your point across. (2) Throw your opponent's tactic back at him by saying, "That was rude of you" or "If you want to take phone calls, perhaps I should come back later." The point with both these approaches is to show your opponent first that you can't be rattled and second that you are on to his tricks. As always, bringing a tactic out in the open effectively nullifies it.

Beware of your opponent trying to make you feel guilty.

When your opponent gives you a hard-luck story and appeals to your "compassion," what he's really saying is that his own negotiating position is a weak one. Examine his appeal carefully—is it carefully staged, or is there really something to it? And how do you wish to respond? With charity, or by moving in for the kill? Only you can decide, but don't let yourself feel pushed into virtue if you feel your offer is still reasonable and if, up to now, your opponent has shown no sign at all of the kindness he is suddenly asking from you.

Beware of the "take it or leave it" ultimatum.

"Take it or leave it" is naked aggression and invites an offensive maneuver. If your opponent so challenges you, tell him point blank that his is not an acceptable negotiating posture. One possible tactic is to simply keep talking as if you didn't even hear what your opponent said. If he hits you with it again, give him an out by suggesting that he misunderstood your position, or that there is another way that would make a negotiated settlement more palatable (perhaps he doesn't realize that money or status is not your only concern). THINK: Before each negotiation begins, always consider what would happen if you did "leave" it—turn down the raise, the offer for your house, whatever. Always have other options ready as a backup.

Beware of your opponent's intention to renege on the negotiated agreement.

If you suspect your opponent might try to undermine or not live up to your agreement, word the agreement in such a way that there is a strong incentive for performance. For example, if he misses a payment he immediately gets hit with an interest penalty. Make it part of the deal that he vacates the scene entirely as soon as you've signed. Or have the settlement progress in steps, each contingent upon the success of the one before. For added insurance, you can bring in a third party to witness the settlement and oversee its execution. But if your opponent is truly sleazy, ask yourself the all-important question: why do I even bother with this bozo in the first place?